D1709002

How Do Alligators Praise the Lord?

Kirk Franklin

Illustrated by Jason Carrier

Charisma
KIDS
A STRANG COMPANY

How Do Alligators Praise the Lord?
by Kirk Franklin

Requests for information may be addressed to:

Charisma KIDS

The children's book imprint of Strang Communications Company
600 Rinehart Rd., Lake Mary, FL 32746
www.charismakids.com

Unless otherwise noted, all Scripture quotations are from the Holy Bible, New International Version. Copyright © 1973, 1978, 1984, International Bible Society. Used by permission.

Children's Editor: Gwen Ellis
Copyeditor: Jevon Oakman Bolden
Design Director: Mark Poulalion
Designed by Joe De Leon and Mark Labbe

Library of Congress Control Number 2004115569

International Standard Book Number 1-59185-209-9
Copyright © 2005 Kirk Franklin
Illustrations copyright © 2005 Jason Carrier
All rights reserved

05 06 07 08 / LP / 5 4 3 2 1
Printed in China

It's those **alligators** praisin' the Lord.

Now what did you say? Is this for real?
Could greasy green gators **get down** and kneel?

I didn't say kneel.
They got no knees!

Gators **roar** their **praise** to the top of the trees.

Look down there. You'll see them raise their great big jaws and **hiss** out praise. **Snouts** to heaven, claws in the bog, and ten-foot tails **drum** time on a log.

and **gold**

and **blue**

and **green**.

They **hum** their **praise** to the **Lord** on high.
They dive to the pond from the sunny sky.

They fly in and **tickle** those gator tongues
and **wave** to the bugs on their slimy gums.

How do catfish **worship?** How do they sail

They **wiggle** their whiskers like
a twangy mouth **harp**
and **sing** the bass line
with big fat carp.

'til he sees a **stump**
and he can duck.

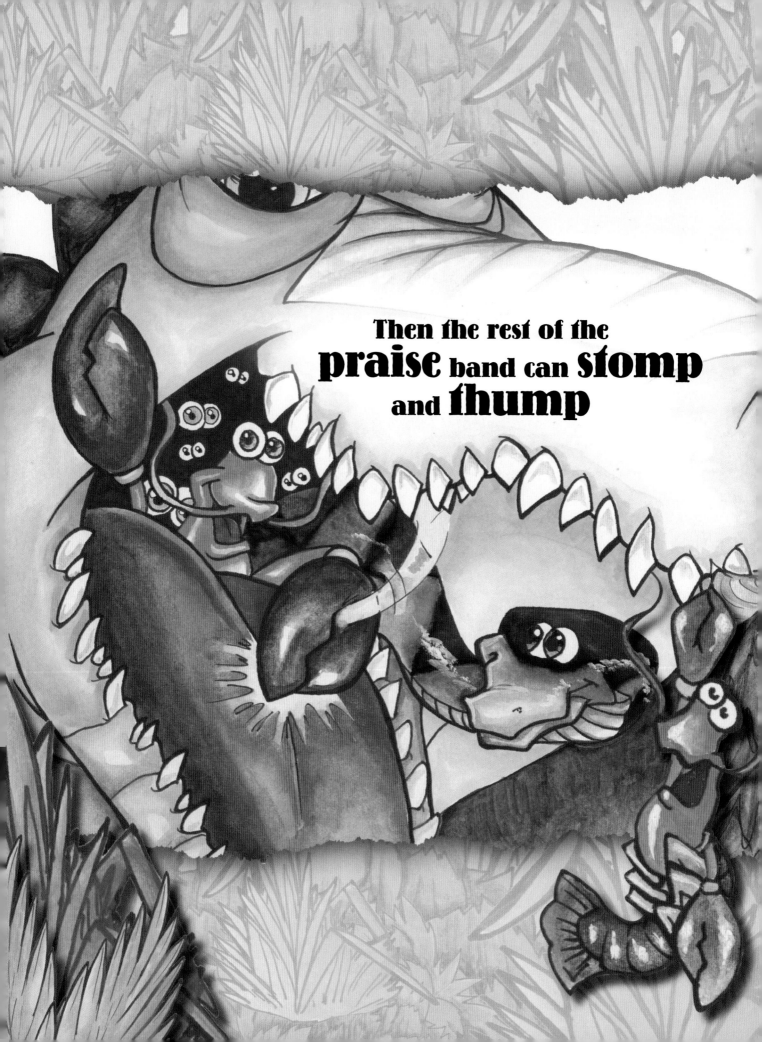

when the gator's **big** jaws are **stuck** on a **stump**.

The door is open, and they **march** on out.
With **praise** for the **Lord**, they **jump** and **shout**.

Crayfish, snails, and waterbugs,
lizards and snakes give each other hugs.